IN THE EVENT

JOHN BIRTWHISTLE was born in Scunthorpe in 1946. His poetry has been recognised by an Eric Gregory Award, an Arts Council bursary, Arts Council creative writing fellowships, and a fellowship at the University of Southampton. His collection *Our Worst Suspicions* was a Poetry Book Society Recommendation. He has had three libretti set and performed; of these, David Blake's *The Plumber's Gift* was staged by English National Opera and broadcast on Radio 3. For twelve years, he was a Lecturer in English at the University of York, teaching mainly the seventeenth century and Romantic periods. From 2012 to 2017, he was a literary contributor and eventually an Associate Editor of the quarterly *BMJ Supportive & Palliative Care*. Birtwhistle is married to a Consultant Anaesthetist and since 1992 he has lived in Sheffield with his family.

JOHN BIRTWHISTLE

in the event

CARCANET

First published in Great Britain in 2020 by
Carcanet
Alliance House, 30 Cross Street
Manchester M2 7AQ
www.carcanet.co.uk

A CIP catalogue record for this book is
available from the British Library.

ISBN 978 1 78410 993 6

Book design by Andrew Latimer
Printed in Great Britain by SRP Ltd, Exeter, Devon

The publisher acknowledges financial
assistance from Arts Council England.

CONTENTS

For my children

Verweile doch, du bist so schön

NOTE

Courrières is a commune near the Belgian border of France. The first coal shaft was sunk there in 1849 and a mining concession was granted in 1852. In 1906, an explosion killed 1,099 miners. On that occasion, German workers came to help rescue their French comrades – the basis for G.W. Pabst's classic film *Kameradschaft* (1931). On 28 May, 1940, an SS division set fire to the village and shot forty-five hostages.

THE PATH TO COURRIÈRES

An 1854 oil sketch by Jules Breton

The gleaner in her shawl, the rough linen sling
at her waist, figured against the evening sky
as she returns to her village, is absent here;
it is the painter himself who trudges home
in the receiving dusk, his harvest done.

The place of the woman is held by the tallest elm,
its crown drawing a scatter of silent rooks.
The path leads the eye peacefully round
to the low houses, brick-red and white,
and to the church tower and beyond.

No hint of surveyors, trial drillings already
there at the time as exploitable veins
were opened and spoil heaps begun. Not yet
the coaldust explosion, the Kameradschaft,
the burning church, the massacred hostages.

Time has scumbled all that history.
I come into the gallery out of the Sheffield rain,
put down my shopping bag next to a bucket
catching the skylight drips. There it is,
its frame a little brighter gold than the corn.

I let my eye be led again by the curve
of the path to Courrières, past the verge
of poppies, the everlasting elm, the wheat
as permanent as Ruth. The rooks, chipped
into the paint, may never settle again.

AN APPEARANCE OF SPRING

In diagonal composure
as though in wood-block print

my daughter   the very person of Spring
stands over me in her slender kimono

as I stoop to the running stream
and reach down to touch   an iris tongue

LIFE-WRITING

A slug is grazing on a flowerpot.

Feeling its way by waves of contraction
it rasps away at layers of green algae

so as to clean a cursive trail of pot-red characters.

It is life, writing.   It is   indecipherable.

THE CORE

The wall I see from my desk where a core
thrown aside has become a blossoming tree
an apple core thrown by the wall
becoming as though to read my thoughts
a small bearing tree
noticed by passers-by who scrump
an apple or share to their friends
its blossom in Spring

shows me this morning a woman so
magnificently pregnant and so
utterly defenceless with laughter
at some story her man insists
on telling her that she has to lean
quaking against the apple-tree wall.
Here's
to the accident that chucked that core!

ANTIQUITY AT ARLES

In a glass case of Roman remains
a neonate is given decent sepulture
in the cradle of a gutter tile.

SPECIMENS OF MAGNOLIA

Almost everyone walking through the magnolia grove
in the Botanical Gardens will take out their mobile.
If alone, they snap a close-up of some selected bloom
and instantly move on. If a couple, they will take snaps
of each other against the blossom and may spend a while
head-to-head confirming whatever it is they have seen.

A daddy taking out his little girls is now phoning
a single perfect flower. His daughters are picking up
fallen petals – pink and pulpy but already rusting
at the edges – and hold them up to each other, using
them as fans, wings, antlers, hats, trying to fly them, until
a squirrel appears and a girl goes chasing after that.

The other stands as still as she can. It approaches her.
It is she who discovers she can write on these petals
with her fingernail and that her scratches will soon turn brown.
And yet, who am I to prefer the less boisterous girl
or my own peculiar lens as I stroll through this grove
to observe magnificent petals preparing to fall?

NOT THAT I ALWAYS NOTICE

For minutes each morning, through
chance alignment of window
staircase and neighbouring trees
a spot of sunlight searches our house,
sometimes so brightly I think
someone must've left on a light.

This morning it casts its own
leafburst onto the kitchen wall
in fluctuant shadows. I open up,
click into My Recent Documents
and catch myself saying aloud:
These may be the best of our days.

AN OAK TABLE

Roses in a pewter jug
Leaden sunset

FROM A JOURNAL OF THE PLAGUE YEAR

Round about now, the clocks change.
Carried over in our diary from year to year,
your note reminds me it is now
that uncontrived woods on the cliff
over Roche Abbey in Maltby Dyke
are sprinkled with wild daffodils
escaping when Capability Brown
brought to order the rest of the ruin.

They are to me as deprivation was
to Cistercian monks who sang.
We'll not be going to look for them;
we have declared it Spring and stuffed
the chimney with a bag of crumpled
news as though a time capsule
because we'll be having no guests.
Soon enough, clocks will change back.

MESSAGE RECEIVED

I had a brush with death this afternoon.
Lost in thought, I thoughtlessly
stepped off the kerb into a contraflow

and a biking courier geared in black
touched me as he slammed to a halt
and cursed me for endangering him.

This angel I apologised and thanked
but he was urgent to be on his way
with notes for persons other than mine.

THE CHOSEN

One of the spirits showed up in human form
although with holes drilled all around his chin
for tying the wisps of straw for his playful beard,
which I found touching so he was the one I asked
Why me? – only to set the others rustling
and whispering amongst themselves how strange
it was that we all ask that: *How strange*
they whispered, *They're always asking 'Why me?'*
Strange that they all ask that. How very strange.

WRITTEN UNDER THE WISTERIA

In memory of Astrid Berthoud

Under the shade of this twining vine
one could sit and look back on the house
from the foot of its long garden and reflect

that the plan had been sturdy, the pergola
firm to support what had to climb
around us to build this arbour of years

and we read her careful signature
of pruning to express the flowers
and persuade the form of their bower

sometimes following best advice,
at others a whimsical snip or weave
of a whippy shoot back into the thicket

of stems which then thicken to branch
and compliantly recall and entwine
a moment's decision into the tangle

of interlaced angle, plash and plait,
each snaking, each harsh truncation
the consequence and living fossil

of someone's thought and action
in long forgotten states of mind
with outcomes, often as not, unforeseen.

Pausing in clearance of the house
to look back once again from this
translucent shelter of memories

I take a long look at the building
from a kitchen chair which itself
is to be one of the last things to go

and study whatever plan or impulse
had been going on there; how the force
of growth will accept and harden choice.

It is not even the annual mass of bloom
but the sombre writhing of leathery stems
that is the really remarkable sight

though May is the obvious floribundance
of dangling of thousands of densely
sweet peas that cluster like so many grapes

therefore best time for estate agents
to picture the house in its peak of allure,
graced as it is by a mature wisteria which

moreover, is sited at the foot of a long garden
that abuts onto a back street, so that this shrub
is easily grubbed to make space for a car.

TREE SURGEONS

Two men dangling in sky
as though on parachutes

shut down chainsaws
fasten their harness

in the chestnut crown
and raise their visors while

birds fall silent and
the sun suffers eclipse.

What is their chat
as a blue cave in a cloud

floats a white canoe?
What does each think

in hushed eerie light
as birds chorus again

and men yank at cords
to re-startle their saws?

DREAMT ENTIRELY IN SOUND

my name   and again   in your voice
a need   sure of the answer yes

THE QUICKENING

a child cups a moth
in her hands – *It tickles!* –

        To hold is to hide

forgotten for years until
        her baby makes

first move

FOR ONE NIGHT ONLY

As I walked alone at night on Port Meadow
She revealed herself as a frail curtain,
The merest breeze gently wavering between
Greenish and pink, so I had to exclaim:
Though so far south, you are the famous Aurora!

I was magnetised by the fold and flow of fabric
As though over the limbs of a goddess
Whose descendant the very next day I enticed
To walk with me at the same place and time
In impious promise of Her apparition again.

TO SEE YOU AS MARTHE BONNARD

flowing so flowingly along your bath
          your flesh the tint of pink champagne
                    dreamily nudging your toe to a tap

as easy with the bathroom door ajar
          as you seem to be with my compare
                    to another man's voluptuous wife

I wonder again at your body's veil

THE AGAVE

In the public park those fleshly limbs
of the Giant Century Plant,
splaying her glaucous rosette
like a Giant Squid, show the scars
of first letters that lovers carve.

ADMIRATION

At the dogtrack a teenager
resting her heel on the bar
clocked my look, so I enquired

Do you do ballet? Her reply,
in its entirety, was
as follows: No.

PROPRIETY

Flopping onto the sofa and kicking off your shoes
is hardly the sort of conduct
one had been lead to expect of The Muse.

THE SLING

It is trying to snow.
Having been ill, my fingers
are thin and white.
Ring slips over knuckle.
The baby slung to my chest
is a clinging monkey.
I am all wrapped up
in her sense of comfort.

THINKING TO TEASE A MAN I THOUGHT A LOUT

I gave into his hand a pebble I'd just found
of granite speckled exactly like an egg
and said be careful how you handle this
and was ashamed by his fine tenderness

STANCES

Our naked boy, fresh from the paddling pool
adopts in purity the Grecian counterpoise,
one thigh forward of his lovely genitals

while his little sister, squatting on the lawn
pulls her comforting tee-shirt from her neck
over her knees and down to her toes

so she makes an Egyptian block statue
presenting a tablet on which to incise
hieroglyphics of ban or of praise.

'WHERE DO YOUR POEMS COME FROM?'

That apple so tartly sweet, the child is surprised
it could grow from the stump of an apple tree

and this crusted old man goes on being surprised
that the very tree could grow from such a pip.

IN WICKSTEED PARK

Clank. The Witch's Hat against its pole. Shouts
keep it turning. Kick the tarmac when it dips, bumps...

A mother watches from a gently swaying swing.

SPLENDOUR IN THE GRASS

Taking a taxi from York station,
the driver taciturn until we arrive
at my tiny front lawn
wildly thick
with seeding grasses and weeds,
he remarks, 'You want a goat.'

One summer when we were little,
we got home from a trip like this
to see our suburban front lawn
was (a word I remember) overgrown –

to parents, reproof to be scotched
at once with the push-mower:
for grass is always neater
on the other side of the fence.

But I was no sooner let out
of the car than I was
rolling over and over on and within
this lovely green
hugging the very grass
I couldn't get close enough to.

Grown a few more years,
the setting light
slanting across a common field,
the glowing yellow light
and the lengthy shadows it cast,
were more intense to me than full day
or the grass as I remember it.

ALL HISTORY WILL BE CLEARED

the name you entered has invalid characters
this program is open but not responding
an unspecified error has occurred
the page you are looking for does not exist
the system has experienced a serious error
do you want to continue? an orphaned file
the file is corrupt and cannot be opened
the page you are looking for does not exist
this message was not sent because of an error
delete all   this action cannot be undone
your return journey time is in the past
this address had permanent fatal errors
the path you entered is too long
this live event is ended   bad gateway
the page you are looking for does not exist

GRATIFIED DESIRE

Lenin thought us Lefties
demonstrate an Infantile Disorder

and here we go again: 'When
do we want it?' – 'NOW!'

THE SEVENTH OF NOVEMBER, 1956

           The sky was violent with shells
tracers and rockets, on Bonfire Night.
                    Next evening, the boy
was indoors tweezing little rubber letters
into the slot of his John Bull Printing Outfit, snipping

rubber into moveable type and paper into strips,
getting confused between S and Z in mirror writing,
and stamping from his pad of violet ink.

                    So in the morning
there he is at the school gate, standing like an orator
on a crate of third-pint milk bottles,
clenching his urgent sheaf and crying BUY
MY NEWSPAPER! ONLY A PENNY!

and, as street newsvendors do, bawling its headline
PORT SAID FALLS!   PORT.   SAID.   FALLS!
– thus giving away, for free, the entire content
of his paper.

          I do not say that Richard Hughes
knew that he was in on the beginning of the end,
or what was then brewing with Russia
or on John Bull's Malayan rubber plantations

but I marvel yet, that this fiery ten-year-old,
not content to impress his own name on his wrist
or make officious tickets for little performances

– this red-headed boy whose message I did not buy

and whom even now I'm ashamed to have teased,
with his penny paper and his triumphant elegy
PORT   SAID   FALLS,   PORT   SAID   FALLS –

was somehow aware that momentous matters
were on the move and the world of Green Lane
County Primary School had to be told that, in print.

VERSE

The young woman opposite me in the train
                    reads a book on the art of poetry.

Would our lives have been so different
                    had I known then what she is learning now?

DESTINY

A heavy trailer has been parked by the playground.
Boys, as they have seen their fathers and brothers do,
kick at the tyres and twang the ropes on the load.

ROCK ART

A child knows at once that to listen
to this story one has only to run
one's finger round and round in the groove

like a gramophone made long ago
by those who knew that cup and ring
fill as today with refreshing rain

SEVA

As a boy on a kerb thumbing a lift
I was addressed by a trim-bearded man
in a turban who gravely beckoned me
into a corner-shop where, with hardly a word,
he presented me with an apple and a shilling.

Was this a natural fatherly impulse of his,
or some ethic, wound into his turban,
expecting neither reward nor result,
or why the distinction? At any rate,
this beggar can still see him now

giving his apple and coin as though to repair
an indignity that he felt for us both.

LAST EVERS

Had two Last Evers today!
Last Ever Religion!!
Last Ever Pee-Yee!!!

And a Last Ever some day
for you my dear
bursting home from school.

CHILDREN CROSSING

The lollipop lady holds up her palm.
I draw up and watch the children cross –
willingly enough, it would seem to me
being screened from their banter.

Silly, but I once applied for her job –
nice hours, cheerful public service –
only to be told with some tact
'It might better suit a pensioner.'

True, I was twenty at the time. Absurd,
held up by children crossing to school,
I still recall that ambition now
that I am so much less disqualified.

AFTER LANGLAND

Please, Holy Church, won't you tell me
Truth?

Daft bonebrain dolt!
It is clear in your youth
little Latin was learned by you.

SON OF GRIEF

See the son of grief at cricket
Trying to be glad.
          A. E. Housman, *A Shropshire Lad.*

If asked which *National Geographic* I most regret
not having stolen from the dentist's waiting room
I should, without hesitation, reply: the one about
cricket, as she is played in the Trobriand Islands

those benighted savages having been taught
by Methodist missionaries the shame to be felt
in nudity and rude ignorance of cricket and Christ,
with the result that these pacific, photogenic folk

to this very day, having feasted, play up the game
kitted out in bright-feathered penis sheaths
and vary somewhat the ritual rules with cries of war
and war dances, and retain on each team a thirteenth man

a marauding jester suitably undressed, whose sole duty
it is to jape about and taunt the foe and sledge
the crowd and send up the whole event. I would like
to tell you more, but just then I was called ▢ not, alas

to the Ministry of the Church, but in to surgery;
yet how often do I muse on those colourful shots
and the difference such thoughtful reforms of the game
might well have made at my Methodist school

where I found myself forever on the boundary
counting (methodically) in a sample square yard,
how many spiders, beetles and such small worms
were also striving to carry on their lives on that ground.

THE QUEEN'S SHILLING

Every year, when exam results are out
so are recruiting sergeants.
School-leavers hanging around
in the city centre, spending money
they don't have on girls they don't have,
are drawn to a small Army tent
with a muted recruitment vid
like a game on pause to be played.
They're talked into the safest of risks
by boy soldiers in combat gear.
This season, the camouflage style
is an effect of sunset on desert sand.

CONTROL OF THE PASS

A track meanders across a brook.
The footbridge could have been held
by some village Horatius from that
pillbox, obstinate for eighty years,
concrete in every sense, mossed-over
and lichen-grey under hard-bitten sky,
with its weighty rust-fastened door
and its slot for postage of grenades.

Waiting in the stuffy blockhouse
to rattle his gun, the bored young man
could so easily've been me or else my son.

THROUGHOUT THE SIESTA

a boy thumps thumps a football
against a Roman wall.

ON A PEBBLY BEACH

When our family was young
and the children took off over the stones like little dogs
as we followed in our different conversation
and the game was, to come back with the Best

it struck me that grownups tend to select
those that the sea had spent her centuries of energy
smoothing and buffing
from rock until perfectly formal, the ovoid, the oval

while our youngsters go for the grotesque,
the knobbly ones with fractured faces and funny holes
that can have fingers poked in and out of them
or look like puppies or gulls

and now that I sleep diagonally
and walk alone on this beach,
it is truly hard to decide
whose preference was the more mature.

CHERRY ON THE CAKE

Having saved the best until last, the child
was too shocked and timid to protest
when the waitress whipped away her plate –
a loss that lingered for the rest of her days.

ON THE NORTHERN LINE

I thought it kinder to take all she wanted to give,
whether a school prize book or a jug with a chip
or several editions of those hefty cotton rope-belted
pyjamas that used to shroud his engendering loins,

which I donated to every bin from my mother's house
to Finchley Central Underground Station,
where the excavators read its gravel to confirm
that the glacier terminates exactly here.

RIDDANCE

Sorting through our parents' stuff,
my sister and I came across
companion Forties paperbacks ▢
The Psychology of Sex
and *The Physiology of Sex* ▢
that gave us a moment's hilarious
relief. Which came first? Which
caused us to come into being?
Which had done us more harm?
Which should we keep? If we're taking
one each, who should get which?
And since, after all, we're talking,
which d'you think I would want?
It was with alarming, vengeful
glee that we hurled both blue
pelicans into the black bin bag.

SIDE LIGHT

Twisting to water
a leaf hesitates

to swirl away

A mountain tip
sails above the mist

METAMORPHOSIS

From Ovid or Bernini one might think
metamorphosis a gentle melt
of one into another form, as though
through animated film from frame to frame.

Not so in nature. There the animal
eats its own innards, discards live limbs,
shatters working tissue, so as to burst
out of its beauteous tegument.

Daphne, morphing to laurel, her pulse
palpable even now through the bark,
is out to trash inheritance

so that a fresh creative form
can erupt, violent as any thought
of Darwin's to our doctrine of fixed kind.

BY DERWENT DAM

Lolling in the dead of summer
      on the bank of a reservoir I watch
         a boy skimming stones
A few skip once and quickly sink
      Mostly they sink at once
         and it looks just lucky when
a stone bounces along like a bomb
      and with the boy Coleridge
         he 'numbers its light leaps'

With no more knack than his
      in duck-and-drake affairs
         I think I can easily see
how he might differ his angle
      select his missiles and govern
         those clumsy energies
except that even as I watch
      he's picking up his own tricks
         and fewer tries go down

utterly into that reservoir
      made by reflected woods
         and by drowned villages

CALLING JAMIE

Helloo! Jamie! Jamie!
You've Wo-on!
You can come out now
The game's o-ver
Brilliant hiding!
We can't fi-nd you
You are The Win-ner
Well done Jamie
Clever clever boy!

It's time to go ho-me
It is getting da-rk
We're going home
Come out Jamie
That's enough now
It's time for te-ea
We've got to go home
We've stopped playing
Come along please

Or we'll go without you!
It's alright Jamie
Are you all right?
No one's angry
Don't be afraid
The hiding's over
Please Jamie please
We're still he-re
We're all getting cold

We never said
We'd go without you
You are our clever boy
You won the hiding game
Can't you hear us
Calling your name?
You can come out now
Wherever you are
Ja-mie! Jamie. Jamie?

EMBLEM

A memory of Sandy Cunningham

As I walked to work across the common
a crow was pecking at a dead rabbit's eye

scared off by a dog who at once addressed
the same matter.

                    In the Common Room
I relate this 'medieval emblem
of bestiality.'

                You merely enquired,
'Why don't you say how human it all is?'

TWO SONGS FROM A MOCK-PASTORAL INTERLUDE

Song of the Shepherd

Calm grove or fluent stream,
Receive my fluid notes compliantly
As the gentle wood-anemone the gentler rain.

Light-fingered breeze, believe
These my liquid sounds as leniently
As a linnet in a linden tree her mate's refrain.

Song of the Gentleman

The very Muses hold this unspoilt glade
In dear regard, and whisper in its shade.
Fed by their springs, the devotee may find
The sweet contentment of a quiet mind.

How fresh it is to leave the harmful air,
The noise and filth and mob, the wear-and-tear
Of London with its rattling wheels and cries
Of trade, the reckless risks, the boasts, the lies.

Here, all the clamour is a flickering dove
And all the busyness is that of love.
Here artless shepherds feed on clotted cream,
Sleep without dreaming for they wake to dream.

'A ROOM IN SAUMUR'
THE PAINTING BY STEPHEN FARTHING

... le théâtre de la vie familiale...
Honoré de Balzac, *Eugénie Grandet*

Knowing as we are about 'the picture plane,'
we hang up our doubts at the door and,
given the title and signs of a room,
try to enter, seek presence or evidence
of actors to live and move in such a space.

We clamber across the fictitious wall
-- though it is too literally dissolved,
leaving sightlines obstructed
by fireback and painting that might
be clarified from this illusion did it not

have deeds to conceal. Foreground clutter
prompts, like forensic tape across a scene,
mingled alarm and complicity
as we feel so bodily enclosed
by what we know delusional.

By now, the story has us by the hair.
What passion held this late household
that empathy should draw us in,
not quite living here but nonetheless
playing along with its emotional tone

which is a cruel, metallic grey?
Why be appalled at the chair punish
-ingly screwed to the floor, forced to stare

at a window form blocked with blank light,
not sky but a screen, switched fiercely on,

or the stagey curtain shapes, all their crimson
of silk of Tours leached away only to steep
to the canvas edges of apron and arch,
into smears we could use to frame an actor,
in view on the frontispiece we'd tried to ignore?

FOR FUTURE REFERENCE

The rippling of reflected sun
on the underbelly of a boat
puts other thought aside

A SIGHTING

She sees

      a sparrow seized
           by a sparrowhawk

She looks around

No one
      had seen it
      but her

RECLINING BUDDHA

A monk, a stigma of saffron,
is walking past a colossal
reclining Buddha.

The drape of his robe reflects
the stone and gathers its folds.
I hesitate

to 'take' a photograph,
to frame the sight as an image,
and I am a snob

about the rack of cards
displaying monks in their robes.
Why snap

him and his impassive
figure alone as though
apart from the flow

of detail such as the cards?
Is it more Buddhist
to contemplate

the process of monk and stone
with no possessive urge
to describe or recall?

Let it all be;
but then how would this
tranquillity

have ever got made,
its 'primitive' style
so aware

of imposing its will upon
the material and within
our passing minds?

The religion began
in distress at our human
suffering,

and for all its technique
of equanimity
brings to mind

cockle-pickers drowning
in the tide of Morecambe Bay
and the witness

– the sound of wind and water
and other foreign voices
shouting and crying –

and the aesthetic sight
of flats of muddy grey
sand speckled

with orange: a tractor,
a tarpaulin, and robes
of saffron monks.

The massively floating form
thinks of Buddha the man
in final illness,

the ineffable word in his smile,
the hand without gesture
pillowing his head.

The monk averts his eyes
from cameras and from
the reclining form.

*The voice of the witness is directly from the emergency telephonist's running
commentary, as transcribed for the inquest at Preston Crown Court (2004).*

TO THE LIGHTING ENGINEER

An argument with Brecht's doctrine of full stage lighting

This is not a theatre
        so we have very few lamps.
The way to play it is restrict
        even those that we have.

Wind down that rig.
        Lower that ceiling still more
so as to sketch in coal
        an adverse area of dark.

As a proper stage can afford
        to sing its aria of light,
we are forced to give over
        most of ours into shade

shadows, musicians
        beggars playing in and out
of such light as is granted
        to characters like ours

as marked by Doré
        the black and white poor
lit infrequently
        by police bull-lantern

or shone up for show
        in magic lantern slides,
but for most of history
        out of light out of mind.

To grant relief
          from dark spotlights,
all other lamps
          being spoken for,

let us devote a single bulb
          a colour-gel a
meretricious peach
          for the tango scene

and look to that glow
          to play upon couples
by way of its glittering,
          its revolving ball.

THE FABRIC OF THE WORLD

A pair of collared doves,
each other's mirror

peck at hawthorn berries
in a pattern of leaves

as though aspiring to print
by William Morris and Co.

LOST FROM HOUSMAN

A stand of beech some fifty strong
Clings to the ridge where it is felled.
That ridge for days the Rifles held.
Who longed to live, did not live long.

NOTICES AT AN EXHIBITION OF RODIN'S DOORS

LASCIATE OGNE SPERANZA
VOI CH'INTRATE

FEEL FREE TO TAKE PHOTOGRAPHS
SHARE YOUR EXPERIENCE

43

ON A CERTAIN POET

That silky cat in a single elegant phrase
draws out the syntax of its motion so as to leave
clear each object cluttered on the mantelpiece it slinks

along and between so as to cause no catastrophe
to obstacles acutely observed and yet un-
touched, leaving things pretty much as they are.

THE RICE WORKERS ARE ON STRIKE

silent paddy fields
    water lilies
        a red flag

SIGINT

The silent aeroplane
A bulge on its forehead
A dolphin's melon

ACADEMIC FEEDBACK

Professor Plagiary! How do you do?
You read my article – how sweet of you.
(Shame that my nourishment did not agree
and you could only spew it back on me.)

ONCE IN BELGRADE

It takes millions of years to petrify wood
by mineral infiltration of every cell.

In an old-style market in Belgrade, I watched
a showman selling whetstones fashioned from
sharp silicate wood-like fibres, a spread of this
matter made up into short rods like so many
carrots. Onto each end, he had forced a length
of heat-softened hosepipe to grip the exact
surface of each piece of stone so as to make
a handle for each tool.

                On with the show.
First, he would noisily deaden the edge
of a pair of scissors with scrapes of the fossil
across each of its shears, then demonstrate
with coarse comedy the thing was now too dull
to cut even one of the squares of newspaper
of which he'd prepared a neat pile. The paper
just got trapped, hardly bruised, the scissors
flaccidly blunt.

Next, with a flourish he seemed
to re-sharpen the scissors with a stick of his own
special wood and, picking up another square
of paper between thumb and forefinger, did not
even try to scissor it but sliced it through in
mid-air with one scissor blade, to show all was now
razor-sharp. Who would not buy fossil wood?

I hung around for several performances
of this perfect pitch, admiring as one might
a conjurer but also thinking, had I to do this all day,
how I might set about it. Perhaps never blunt
the scissors – just appear to, with dramatic
swordplay, loosening the pivotal rivet
so edges could never engage. Then, for the
aerial display, have to my hand that blade,
ready-sharpened, as it might well have been,
by some private source of fossil wood.

So musing
sceptically, but also relishing his art, I was not
the only one to notice that, deliberately
or not, the very next square on the pile of news
happened to frame exactly a standard press
portrait of Tito.

The watchers fell strangely
attentive, but the artist showed not the slightest
sign of clocking the icon. He followed routine
until that point where he would have slashed
the image on the next square of paper which,
however, without fuss, he carefully laid aside.

Or so I remind in mineralising memory.

AN ENTREPRENEUR'S PROGRESS

It having seemed, in '68, a cool idea
to plant an unkempt traffic island

with 'grass' for harvest at night,
the suspended sentence taxed

the wit of red-top headlines
– TOFF SWINGS FOR ROUNDABOUT –

amused by his V to the rules
his kind lay down for us herd.

Shown on Personality shows
as a young meteor (to mean

a quick streak of attention
not the burn out and fall), that

was that; until he spotted
in the crack of a pavement

with groundsel, a few stalks
of alien barley in full ear,

a gesture planted to shock
for a sec the hurrying man.

A nearby poster was, after all,
already defaced, half torn-down

with its quote from Guevara – *il faut
s'endurcir, sans jamais se départir*

de sa tendresse – and its feeling,
its assured pen drawing,

of an unbroken ear of barley,
the grain arising from the stem

as letters in a sensitive hand,
the tines of the nib gently splayed

to fill out the seed, then relaxed
to whisker off into a trailing line

the world now knows as his Logo
stamped on goods of every kind.

He started with us. He began
with paper packets of grain

given away at demo and festival
to take home and disrupt

the routine illusion of parents
about their daily drudgery.

He never did find out which
hippy pacifist had drawn this, his

perfect trademark, but once colour
supps had featured the brand

as a quirk for gardens bizarrely
involved with bootleg music,

he swung into orbit. Thence
the wholly natural cosmetics,

the expensive parodies
of market-stall knockoffs,

the no-frills conveyancing,
the private jet to private island,

the wives, the girlfs, the laddish
charm that gets it off and away,

the creative accounting, the smile,
the brilliant bankruptcies, the tax

frauds of THE ANARCHIST KNIGHT,
the SPIRIT OF FREE ENTERPRISE.

THAT WE ARE ALL MEMBERS OF
ONE ANOTHER

as a theorem of Set Theory
makes complete sense to me.

AT THE BARBER'S

Mr Scott used to work at the chair with the best light
and a view of the street to keep an eye on regulars
as we went about his business of growing our hair;

If we noticed him as we passed he'd raise a scissor,
patient that we'd soon enough be back through his door.
Well turned out, his own hair low-maintenance,

a military-looking man, I thought he'd outlast me.
Epochs of daytime television passed over his head
as he'd clip, chat, and keep a watch on the street.

How're the children doing? I still call them that.
How's the mother getting along? You know how it is.
How many grandkids does that make? His restless

motion back and forth round the back of the chair
was continually wearing out a grooved arc
not only through the lino but into the very boards

as though he might drop like the cartoon fisherman
through a hole he'd sawn for himself through the ice.
I didn't know he'd gone till I saw the new lino.

IN THE STYLISH LAMP

white and frosty as mint-cake,
lie carcasses of flies

'BALLIOL MEN STILL IN AFRICA'

Deplorable, I would agree.
But what of all those Balliol men
              still in Balliol?

OF THE NINETY AESCHYLEAN TRAGEDIES

only seven survive. Good grief;
what could the rest have prompted us to?

JOHN BRADFORD, EXECUTED 1555

He that said   *There but for*
the Grace of God go I   went.

IN THE CHIPPY

for Dimetrios

The young Cypriot in the chippy
displays on his arm a skilful tattoo,
a bearded face with flowing mane.

I ask him, which of the gods is that?
Hercules. But surely, Hercules
should be wearing the skin of a lion?

At which he swivels like a dancer
and there on the back of his arm
is The Nemean Lion as ever was.

As he turns again to crozzling fish
and a wire basket of chips, the whole
shop smells of olive, lemon and wine.

THE BEST EXCUSE I EVER HEARD

was a poem in itself.

          My chameleon
adapted herself to our Persian carpet
so that my sister couldn't see it and trod on her
so that I had to take it to the chiropractor
and that

      is why I couldn't come to your tutorial

A DUTCH INTERIOR

A lady in blue in an inner room.
A being that one fed on cactus might see
as an angel, a pure concept of light.

The household knows a letter's arrived.

The cook has her eye to the keyhole,
having quelled the puppy with an egg.
On a cleanly tile, slimy edges of egg.

The lady hesitates to break the seal.

The maid, to show herself unslovenly,
swishes the floor. In the trail of her broom
the dust resettles itself into gentle drifts.

AN INQUIRY INTO THE PORTRAIT
OF JOHN WHITEHURST
BY JOSEPH WRIGHT OF DERBY

In memory of Mark Roberts, Conservator

He is discovered in his study at night.
His astute, unflattered profile,
the hair thinned through tracts of time,
looks up slightly, as though to weigh
an idea that's just entered his head;
two other themes being lit: his work,
overflowing the writing slope, and,
through the window of his Grand Tour,
a distantly smouldering Vesuvius –
one of Wright's tenebrous Italian views.
Otherwise, timeless abstract night.

Such a tableau was easily read
by the worthies of Derby. It displays
a finding by their ingenious friend
who by dint of diligent reason
adds to the sum of useful knowledge.
The paint renders, almost to touch,
not only his gently capable face
but his thought: the crucial diagram
of local strata known to owners of mines,
which they possess in copperplate, folded
into their fifteen-shilling quartos of

I N Q U I R Y

INTO THE

ORIGINAL STATE AND FORMATION

OF THE

E   A   R   T   H ;

DEDUCED FROM FACTS AND THE LAWS

OF NATURE.

At last! a product from all those years
of listening to him at the table, his face
in candlelight, the clock of his own
making on the mantelpiece as he
sorted and measured his day
-by-day observations in Matlock.
Here at last every wheel is in gear
and this the great connection he drew.

He is discovered in deep shadow,
with not even a clock to suggest
the slightest sound, for this
is the primal scene, the fertile night
bringing the unforeseen into birth.
The paper, the volcano and the man
are placed as in a waking dream,
all else in suspense. And, for a study,
not a book is visible to show
the natural philosopher the way,
or the world how it comes to be as it is.

But, if this be illumination,
there is no saint or poet's eye
rolling in frenzy to inspiring source:

He is alert but level. He looks up
slightly from his work, to consider
a thought in distance out of the frame.
Oh, I see! It's exactly the way a painter
glances up to check his subject.
Wright, in depicting his friend,
depicts him as a brother artist
as he brushes that thinning hair.

In the very instant of insight,
the painter compacts his own volcano
with his friend's precise drawing
of a section of local habitat
prepared for the engraver's burin.
It is a painting about the moment
of thought, about art, about science,
and it paints about friendship.
It is a painting about the stubborn
intensity of loving attention
that may elicit concept from dark.

He is discovered in his study like Faust
in Goethe's Rembrandt frontispiece,
riddling forbidden mines of lore,
the toadstone nodules and the rifts
loaded with ore that conjure
rules of stratigraphy, Vulcanism,
the subterranean fire, the inferno
indifferent to us as the planet revolves
within the clockwork orrery.
His book will clarify Creation, the point
of his pencil turned to his own breast.

ON A DETAIL IN AN IMAGINARY PAINTING

We can read the signs that the frail boat
hardly moves. Its tether is curving slack.
It forms no ripple on the harbour pool.

Roped to a rusty chain, by lobsterpots
– heaped ribcages one almost smells –
it looks as accidental as it could be.

So what is it convinces us that she
was moored up then and there
just as painted, at that time of day?

It has everything to do with light
falling coherently across the scene
to shadow volumes of net and hull

but why should it also make us think
of unstaying things that cannot be moored,
yet stay when we ourselves are no more?

'CROUCHING VENUS'

As crouching marble makes
the goddess use her hands
elbows, knees and their soft hinges

draw attention to those parts
of her body she affects to hide,
so (the white line of stanza-

break serving that simile) our art
must conceal its art although
not too well; for how much art

was made except by fighting shy
of those without whom not
one of us was brought to light?

ON A MINIATURE BY ANTON WEBERN

An initial letter
    glowing with knowledge

Exacting as light
    that glances about within cut glass

As exposed as a fact
    that gives itself no excuse

Yet close, open and closed,
    as the locket held to your breast.

ONE SINGING

Upstairs you are singing bit by bit
   testing your part against
     the odd piano note

going methodically round
   and around as a bee
     its foxglove.

I catch a fine instance.
   I pour with logical joy.

REVIEW

Designs unfulfilled - so what?
     So many follies not done.
Books promised, unwritten?
     So many fewer words to eat.
Comforts disconsolate
    to any artist or lover.

THIS NOVEMBER MORNING

Although my time is running out, I'll not
give up adjectives or twist or fact.
I'll stick to these intricacies of frost.
The 'late bare style' I Ieave to my bones.

WISDOM

The Chinese thought a pen, an idea
and a long life were all a scholar needs.
Luckily, I'm blessed with both of these.

DWELLING ON LI PO

I read again an ancient poem about a man that had for company
        a stalk in a vase, a cup of wine and the pendulous moon.

My flowers are dead, the wine empty and even that moon
        is behind a cloud. I am washed over by knowledge

that my friend has gone away at last into his own country.

I suppose one day when I can hardly walk to the point
        and to clamber out of my bath is an evolutionary stage

and I'm ringing a man to ask whyever the light
        on/off gismo thingy seems to be going awry

that I'll still imagine I'm faffing around with poems like this

searching again and again for that age-old precision
        wherein an elderly man drank himself into solitude

with a cup, a twig of blossom and this evening's full rising moon.

*Li Po, 701–762 AD, great poet of the Tang period. A typical poem was
translated by Arthur Waley as 'Drinking Alone by Moonlight' (1919).*

FROM THE STREAM

I pick up a stone
streaming with iron arteries

I let it fall back

A FALLACY

Although there can be
   no such thing
      as a 'poetical' subject

the woods refine
   drifts of light
      at rest on our path

AN ARCHAEOLOGIST EXPLAINS A SCAR

This shallow bowl's ineffaceable trace
was not just another charcoal-burner's pit:

mounded along this edge, depleted over there
from soil being ripped up and transferred,

it is that a great tree once fell in these woods,
tearing to drag upright its webbed foot grasping

at stones, only to rot and release them over the years
to leave this crescent for us to interpret, exclaim

how mighty a column it was that long ago crashed
and how shallow it must always have been, in its roots.

SPECIAL COLLECTIONS

I had only to sign the forms, and forms
he touched were rendered into my hands.
In the reverent silence of that special vault
I spent a whole day leafing remains
of a well-known poet I had slightly known.

All there, all missing, they conserved
the doodles, the thousands of starts,
the odd pocket of naughty rhymes and
the teasing spores, happy dust of research,
that brought about a garlanded poem.

Recollecting him as he once gave to me
a glimpse of these same 'foul papers'
I began to sense a murmur from the page:
John, yes it's me, Frank, talking to you.
Never permit this if you have any sense.

Keep on writing your harmless poems
but keep yourself from unfeeling eyes.
Although we spawn prolific as salmon, if
as we scribble we pay the slightest thought
to such designs they parch on the bank.

We're good but not Goethe. Don't revere
your own relics. Our widows have other resorts.
What I have not written I have not written.
Therefore I stay up late sorting bales of paper
for rough men to collect from recycling bins.

ON A GUIDED TOUR

Here we are, in the renowned Spiegel Café,
scene of the last poem before he shot himself.
Yes, all these mirrors are great for selfies.

This is the actual corner seat where he watched
via those mirrors the demented gentleman
– Do grab yourselves a coffee while you can –

whom the regulars dubbed The Professor
who'd sit all day long with endless pots of tea,
soundlessly declaiming to his imaginary class

– and don't miss out on the legendary gâteaux
drenched in liqueur, though in our poet's day
the Spiegel was, as it were, more bohemian.

You can take it in turns to sit exactly here
and I'll go round the corner so you can spy
on my reflection pretending to mime,

as in the poem, rhetorical touches of passion,
intense gazes from side to side of the room,
and the pause with courteous gesture to attend

to some objection unheard from the floor,
mouthing an answer self-pleased at its wit,
acknowledging ripples of silent applause.

Or you can take yourself, if it strikes you
as amusing, in one of his dumbshow faces:
the sceptical eyebrow, the signature smirk

pointed out in countless engravings that we
half noticed as children, regarding the past
as it was insisted upon us in those days.

And of course you see written on mirrors
in every language the final stanza,
perhaps a little pretentious to our taste,

about the mercurial mirror as the very image
of such lucidity as may... But you know the phrase.
And how, unless ironical, our poet claims

to envy that pathetic café Professor,
lecturing to thin tobacco smoke, his air
of simple-minded contentment with words

oblivious to any present audience. We now
have a few minutes to eat up and take snaps.
Then the coach will take us to look at his grave.

SWEET OUSE RUN SOFTLY

A motorboat roars by

Seconds later its wash
flaps against the shore
for a few seconds

Run softly, sweet Ouse

TO EVERY THING THERE IS A SEASON

A time to join up, and a time to resign;
             a time to weed, and a time to pot out;
A time to bury, and a time to disclose;
             a time to collect, and a time for the charity shop;

A time to research, and a time to write up;
             a time to stay put, and a time to set forth;
A time to concede, and a time to demur;
             a time to freeze, and a time to microwave;

A time to conceive, and a time to abort;
             a time to print, and a time to shred;
A time to recycle, and a time to repair;
             a time to vote, and a time to abstain from voting;

A time to cling, and a time to release;
             a time to wed, and a time to divorce;
A time to judge, and a time to tolerate;
             a time to advise, and a time to withhold advice;

A time to assemble, and a time to disperse;
             a time to measure and a time to cut;
A time to be vague, and a time to define;
             a time to swim, and a time to give up swimming.

SOME PROPERTIES OF 'VANITAS PAINTINGS'

The child's globe; the descant recorder,
emblem not of deathless art
but mortal shortness of breath;

drosophila, that ephemeral
lab animal that flirts around
our bowl of ripening fruit;

those shards of clay pipe we found
in the soil, last touched by lips
of men who built this house,

kept on our sill as though to remind
of Jeremy Taylor's words that we
are but dreams of shadows of smoke;

even the half-spent candle,
its melting tears at its flank,
at the ready to time a power cut;

and my wife's skull, the one she studied
at medical school, procured from Hell
knows what killing fields;

but then: the children's delight
at a dandelion clock shooes away
all my bats and owls.

IN TIMES OF PESTILENCE

When the Black Death came scything through Florence
Boccaccio had his ten narrators
in islands of villas whiling away
the greatest ever boxed set of stories.

When the same angel winged into Cambridge,
Newton holed up in Woolsthorpe manor house
and spent the time under an apple tree
forming his universal idea.

It is a plague year but nothing occurs
to me. The buses go lit but empty
while 'cattle come home to their barns at night
without keepers, as though rational beings.'

Quotation from Giovanni Boccaccio, The Decameron, *Introduction to the First Day.*

SILVER BIRCH

Clear in cobweb,
wings of seed.
All over, in fact.

We tread them
into the house,
they sleep in our folds.

Primal woodland here,
did we die
or desert it, silver

birch would succeed
as though our kind
had never breathed.

AT SWINE STY, 1ST JULY 2020

The valley turns, and in this hollow
the breeze has fallen. A lark descends.
The fragrant bracken is nearly still.
A solitary foxglove hardly sways.
Deer tracks converge in shelter.
High and around are Bronze Age fields
abandoned to the sky.
All the senses will have been so then.
                                        How voices carry!

AN INSIGHT

Being shown an x-ray of my own
writing hand, I felt a twinge of awe
at tracery like any east window.
The fracture was clear enough, but so
were interlaced structures I came away
bound to try and make something of –

not of myself, but still worthy of that
gray-scale elegance the screen
revealed to me. Which is why
this pricking bone in my hand
is a wishbone that spurs me to wish
my bones a little longer articulate.

THE CARE-BED

We have made her bed in the living room.   *this is not a comfy bed*

There are flowers, amongst them yours.   *let me be*

There are bowls of fruit, lively as flowers   *in my own bed*

In a place of laughter and of argument.   *cot rails I know the make*

They say that each of us holds one book   *dear boy he died in it*

Inside them. We are reading hers now.   *there are rooms*

We are writing out a long scroll   *where I am already dead*

From all she recalls of her family tree.   *please*

She is in an old house where the walls   *let me do it*

Understand these comings and goings.   *these are not*

It is not silent, it is profoundly quiet.   *my belongings*

There are few words, amongst them yours.   *why are you singing?*

The hearth has heard it all before.   *I am not in Hell*

Her bed is made in the living room.   *why are you singing like that?*

TO ONE WHO TOOK HIS OWN LIFE

Oak leaves and catkins are fluent again
along the branches you no longer see,
your mind and mine held forever awry.

Struck by a curious line of poetry –
my first thought being to share it with you,
were you not mining inaccessible seams.

I hear a son's concert in his father's name.
We knew both violinists. Where were you?
Involved in staring down a deep stairwell.

How to reply, when you told me delight
had drained from painting and only cows
are content to chew on landscape beauty

and music itself was turning ugly by
a labyrinthine disease of the ear?
We spoke of the Heiligenstadt despair.

Had I been with you to stare down that well,
would I've asserted Beethoven kept up his fight,
or laid down my thoughts along with yours,

or tried to restrain you? You have your own spark
I cannot stand by and watch you snuff out.
About this I am not stoical, nor will I cheat

by taking us back to those catkins as though
recurrence felt like renewal. I set myself
to think, as did you, how to stare all this down.

Which sounds too much like a last line.
I hope I could simply have stood at your side
so that you were not quite so utterly alone.

VERSIONS OF FOUR JAPANESE *JISEI* WRITTEN ON THE VERGE OF DEATH

I have no house   no wife   no child
no wooden printing block
no money   yet I wish for no death
   Shihei Hayashi (1738–1793)

A dewdrop came and went
Once I governed Osaka
    that dream of dreams
   Hideyoshi Toyotomi (1536–1598)

I wish my life to end
 under cherry blossom
  at the full February moon
   Saigyō Hōshi, (1118–1190)

Wherever has that dog got to?
I thought of him again
tonight as I came to bed
   Shimaki Akahiko (1876–1926)

ORDERS OF BURIAL

Driven from the city to its rim of hills
that give onto the distant plain,
our black cars slow to walking pace,
make sense of the gradient slump
so the body knows we are going down.
At this, having been lost in our thoughts,
we think we've arrived, look around,
but vista has straitened to a narrow lane
descending close domineering walls
as though we tunnelled a Pyramid.

The convoy issues at the foot, the same
slot of horizon now defined
by black avenues of cypresses.
Family alight and set about their work.
It feels wrong, glancing back to observe
how the trick had been engineered.
Behind us, severely parallel walls
concrete-buttressed against the slope
like the flume from a dam, had cast
the extreme cleft that had taken us in.

For those of us still able to leave,
the original route's never taken again;
that remorseless mock defile,
that bodily sinking, has caused
once and for all its ennobling fear.
Here they will rent his short plot
and return every year to touch, to kiss
the enamelled photograph and leave

every tint, from white to orange to rust,
of chrysanthemums to dry in the sun

until the very last day for which
the cheque was signed, whereupon
his remains are unearthed, crushed
and pigeonholed into an ossuary
tiled with numbers and names,
whom I last saw in the hospital
and, lightly on his temple, kissed
when he asked that the reading lamp
over his pillow be switched off by me,
murmuring *La piccola luce... Spegni.*

BY THE WAY

the corpse

   of a stolen purse

emptied
   thrown aside

THE SAME

a frail
faded poppy

daylight
moon

'WHERE'S THE POETRY IN THAT?'

– as he used to demand of his students.

*E.A. (Archie) Markham (1939–2008) wrote
under various names, including 'Sally Goodman'*

I bumped into your old flame Sally at the shops.
I was palpating an avocado when this hand
appeared. I knew her from that kitchen scar.
'Are they ready?' 'Ripeness is all,' I quipped.
She had the courtesy to laugh, drawing herself
up into that lengthy Scandinavian beauty
you used to say was in so many ways like you.

I started to tell her how deeply I missed...
She started to say 'These days I scarcely exist...'
We lapsed into reminiscent silence.
We knew the other knew the anecdotes.
So I dared to ask, 'What did he really believe?'
'He believed: that Lucy Locket lost her pocket.'
With that, she faded up the Fresh Food aisle

leaving me still half looking out for you
bowling towards me with your dandy red
scarf streaming against the wind, drafting
to yourself the line of this morning's
sulphurous fissure, sadly provocative yet
true all the same, as in your saying 'And so
friends die to help us bring forth poems.'

The last ten words are from Markham's A Rough Climate *(2002).*

'I SING A RAINBOW'

for Archie

Along the empty streets, unseen children
are encouraged to display their paper
rainbows to lift up our hearts. Some obey
the analysis of Newton's prism;
some the strict order of mnemonic song,
bridging its 'purple and orange and blue'
as well as, seditious to nature, 'pink.'

Funny for idle hands, maybe harmless enough;
but is this idea that flies its flag on town halls
not a little too pure? It is light celestial,
not reflected from worldly pigment.
Children array its colours each as distinct,
with no shade or intermingling tint,
and wash the brush between every band.

But in still other windows, infantile arms
smear in arcs every hue and cry in the box
without order of precedence or shame
at muddy colours that paints really make:
natural fingers, woody and streaked
as well as black, that solid void, that
spectral line of an element unknown.

THANKS TO BASHŌ

Bashō did not invent the long tradition of *haiku* but he brought it to perfection. By the late seventeenth-century, however, the immense associations compressed into such a tiny form stood in need of commentary.

A literate caste brought up with its codes had no need of context; context needed to be made explicit only when such assurances were breaking down.

Bashō had expected to become a modestly secure samurai but was thwarted in that career by the death of his patron.

Thus he became a professional writer dependent on disciples and on those who valued his commentary at literary events. Their cultivated hospitality was a fixture of his restless journeys.

The cryptic eloquence of his poems, their pretence of self-sufficiency, their sense of nature, the peculiar poignancy which some other cultures have found so agreeable, harked back to a hierarchy which had supported the poet.

It is therefore reasonable that, so far from relying on his poems as compact pods of meaning, Bashō so often lead his readers into them through highly crafted prose.

Bashō's prose is of four overlapping kinds.

One consists of critical remarks, such as his judgements in poetry contests which imply tenets of writing.

A second is the explanatory headnote.

A third is narration, usually about one of his journeys, which may set the context for a *haiku* but also offsets it poetically.

And fourthly there are his *haibun*, or brief prose introductions which are as considered as the poems themselves, which share some *haiku* techniques and to which the ensuing poem relates in ways that have affinities with its internal relations.

As a hiker, I am looking mostly not at the landscape but at my feet. Which is to say at the thought processes of other walkers, such as goats.

How they have expanded the path and its erosion by walking in parallel to a slightly lower path which had become too squelchy.

How the stone or stick dropped in the boggiest place is a record that someone put it there to help himself.

Yet also, how it helps me across an awkward spot.

If we find such aids across the mire, it follows that someone has gone before and left them for us underfoot.

Bashō wrote in elements of two or three lines.

The landscape of his very last poem is a blasted moor.

In his *renku* 'Summer Moon,' he had described one's footsteps across a marsh being aided by farmers in poor land who had laid planks over the worst of the quag.

On a high lonely moor, tradition. A curlew's call, curlew, curlew.

The centuries. The morning.

That glint on a curlew's wing.

That exact mood of loneliness which is set up between a frail creature or event and the surroundings by which it could well be overshadowed, but to which this very mood might show it to connect.

To find a few timbers carefully laid down. A precursor.

What is friendship? A common taste in poetry.

> a desolate moor
> grasses trembling in the wind
> these two or three sticks

AN HUMBLE PETITION TO THE FAIRY OFFICERS

Well into the last century, Irish country people had an explanatory framework for mental 'alienation' that was at least as coherent as anything proposed by the medicine of their time; namely, that the afflicted person had been exchanged or 'taken' by the Fairies.

Potent bewildering kindly Sirs,
Inspirers of springs, hidden lords
Of milking and crops, arbiters
Of sea-peril and in music supreme;

We, a family at wits' end, entreat
Your honoured ears to our petition:

That, after such interval as may please
Your Graces, you graciously restore
Our child to his family and powers.

As to our boldness in addressing
Your high persons, we can only plead
We have been at every pain to consult
Philosophers wise in such things

And not one has a better thought
Than you have spirited our son away
To enjoy your hospitality awhile;
So great, so undeserved a privilege

That, grateful, we request you name
Any consideration in clinking coin
Or buttermilk or finest flour of oats
Or eggcups brimming with potcheen

To be left by whatever threshold,
Well, lost shoe, thorn bush
Or rare isolated flower that you
May be pleased to designate.

Have we offended your ways,
Be gentle to clarify the cause
And resolve amicably; for
Do we not live on the same land?

We are already knocking, stone
By stone, our most recent barn
Lest it had unwarily blocked
Some natural lane of yours

For this, his family, truth to tell,
Is pining with grief to see him again
As once he was, charming, self-
Possessed as you have him now.

We are growing to accept it may
Please your Excellencies to prolong
The honour of his sojourn with you
For a far while yet in our time.

You will find him clever company,
Knowledged in the kinds of fiddle;
Just ask him to chat about his cat
Or traveller's tales in democracy.

May we, however, with respect,
From out of merely human hearts
Invite you to weigh in intellect:
That he was not raised in your world

And may hanker for primitive ways.
His father, mother, sister, friends
Yearn for his pleasing fellowship,
Wherefrom we fully appreciate

That your Graces will be entranced
By his comely discourse and person
Who may even begin to think
Yours is the world he wishes to live;

And yet, discerning as you are,
You may come to tire of human style
In horsehair drawn across catgut,
So unlike what it has been our luck

To catch, on rare evenings, floating across
The stony mist, faint sound of, your
Ingenious music in solemn revels
At respectful distance from your fort.

His dancing figures may be strange
To you as glimpses of yours are to us,
So might there perhaps come a day
When your Reverends, now entertained

By your curious courtier, feel surfeit
Of his society and, in your noble tact,
Enquire whether he is wholly content
To be so away from his own music?

May your gentle natures pardon
Laughable clumsiness of form
In little folk approaching you thus,
Our being illiterate of any court

Or cogent precedent likely to move,
Or proper manners to address,
Such authority as yours, deferring
Solely to your rights in the matter

Which is to us no less than the joy
Of our dearly beloved young man

Whom we have the temerity to implore
That you may give us leave to hope
That some day without cloud or omen

Just as he disappeared, we shall see
Again, smiling and playing on his violin.

ACKNOWLEDGEMENTS

Many of these poems were first tried out in Sheffield at readings for The Broomhill Festival or Writers in the Bath, and I thank those audiences. Two appeared on the Manchester Writing School's online project *WRITE where we are NOW*. Three were printed in *PN Review* 254. 'Thanks to Basho' was published on *The Bow-Wow Shop*. The versions of Japanese *jisei* were made with the help of Keizo Shimizu and printed with my commentary in *BMJ Palliative & Supportive Care* (February 2017). The 'Two Songs from a Mock-Pastoral Interlude' are extracted from my libretto for David Blake's opera *The Plumber's Gift*.

Under the 2020 virus lockdown, I published and commented on a few of these poems for The Broomhill Festival at http://www.broomhill-festival.org.uk/john-birtwhistle and read one for Derby Museum & Art Gallery at https://www.derbymuseumsfromhome.com/activities/poetry-in-lockdown.

The paintings by Jules Breton and Stephen Farthing are in the Graves Gallery, Sheffield, and Joseph Wright's portrait of John Whitehurst is in the Derby Museum & Art Gallery. These can all be found on the Art UK web catalogue. A paradigm of the 'crouching' type of Venus (or Aphrodite) is a Roman copy of one by Doidalsas of Bithynia, in the Vatican.

As always, I am grateful for the genial criticism of Alan Brownjohn, Jack Donovan, Michael Glover, Hugh Haughton, Trevor Stacey, Tim Webb and my family.

Go, little book

and find your way

to unknown friends